PIANO STARTERS

VOLUME ONE
by Carol Barratt

This book is dedicated to my son Jody

Pages 2-3 separate hands
pages 4-7 alternating hands
pages 8-16 hands together

This book © Copyright 1984, 1990, 1995 Chester Music.

Illustrations by Sarah Lenton
© 1995 Sarah Lenton.

Chester Music Limited
(A division of Music Sales Limited)
14/15 Berners Street, London W1T 3LJ

STARTERS

5 4 3 2 1

AIR DES BOUFFONS

From a French Folk Tune

MARCH OF THE PIGS

WHEEEEEE — WHIZZZZ

WHUMP!

AU CLAIR DE LA LUNE

French Folk Tune

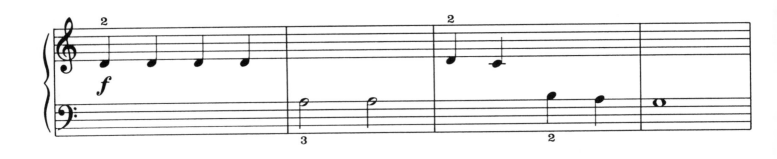

BALLOONING

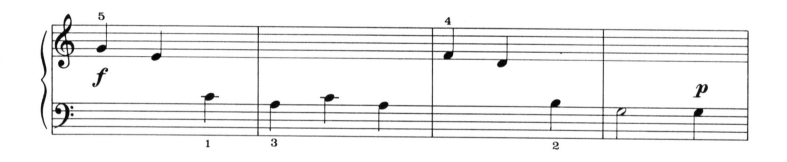

6

THREE NURSERY RHYMES

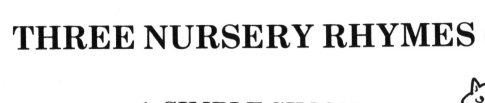

1. SIMPLE SIMON

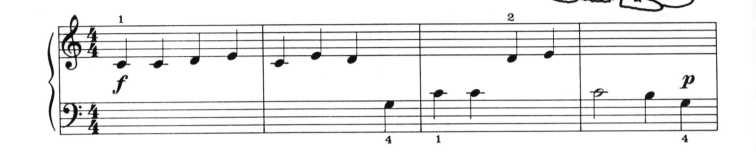

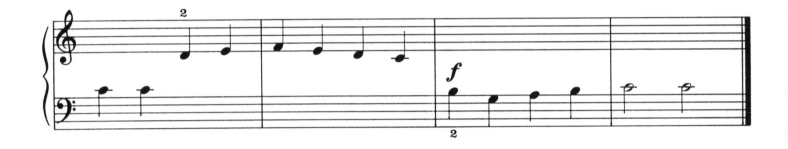

2. LONDON BRIDGE IS FALLING DOWN

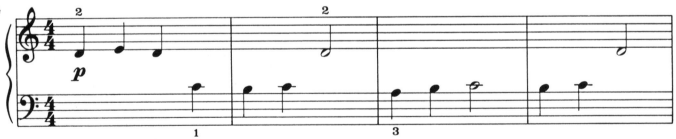

Watch out here

3. PUSSY CAT, PUSSY CAT

8

RAGTIME

Hands Together!

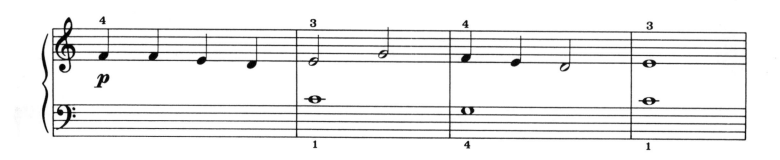

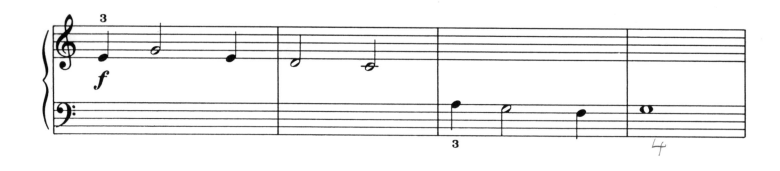

Both hands!

WALTZ FOR DIDDLES

EXERCISE TIME

EVENING SONG
Spot the rests

German Folk Tune

RESTING!

LULLABY

Welsh Folk Song

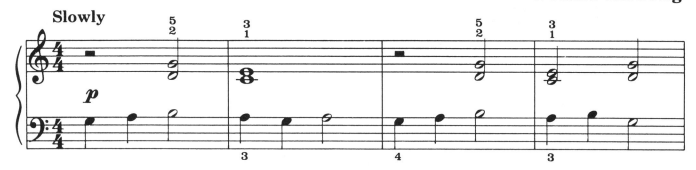

OLD WOMAN

American Folk Song

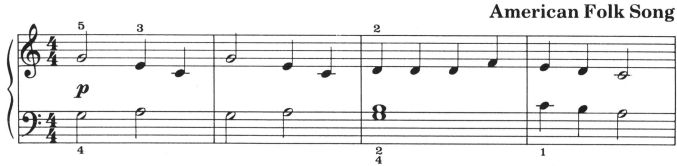

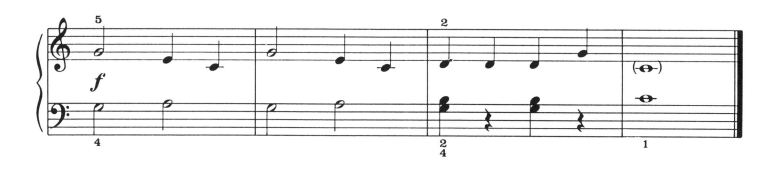

This piece is called...

J'AI DU BON TABAC
Spot the B♭'s

French Folk Song

OFF TO WORK

14

RIGADOON
Spot the F♯'s

From H. Purcell

COSSACK DANCE

Lively

HOT CROSS BUNS

Don't forget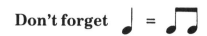

Traditional

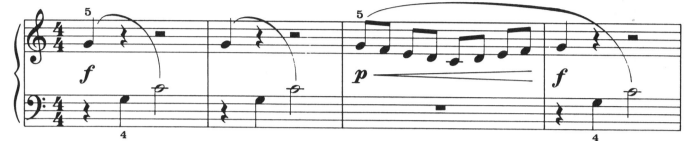

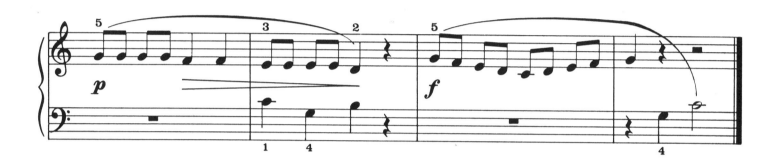

ORANGES AND LEMONS

Watch out

Traditional

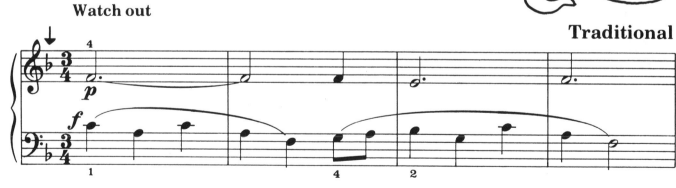

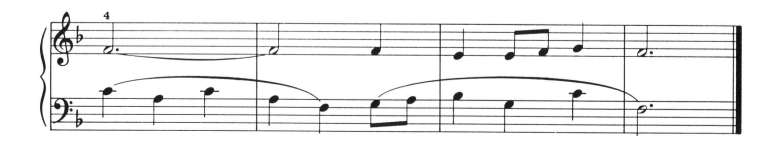

JODY'S CAKE WALK

Printed and bound in Great Britain by
Caligraving Limited Thetford Norfolk

1/09(168518)